The New Testament

ALSO BY JERICHO BROWN

Please

Jericho Brown

The New Testament

 Copper Canyon Press
Port Townsend, Washington

Cover art: Léon Bonnat, *Le Barbier nègre á Suez*

Copper Canyon Press is in residence at Fort Worden State Park in Port Townsend, Washington, under the auspices of Centrum. Centrum is a gathering place for artists and creative thinkers from around the world, students of all ages and backgrounds, and audiences seeking extraordinary cultural enrichment.

LIBRARY OF CONGRESS CATALOGING-IN-PUBLICATION DATA
Brown, Jericho.
[Poems. Selections]
The new testament / Jericho Brown.
  pages cm
ISBN 978-1-55659-457-1 (paperback)
I. Title.
PS3602.R699A6   2014
811'.6—dc23

                                    2014018141

Copper Canyon Press
Post Office Box 271
Port Townsend, Washington
98368

www.coppercanyonpress.org

In memory of
Messiah Demery
(1981–2008)

ACKNOWLEDGMENTS

Earlier versions of these poems appeared in the following journals and anthologies: *44 on 44: Forty-Four African American Writers on the Election of Barack Obama, 44th President of the United States*, The Academy of American Poets' *Poem-A-Day*, *The American Poetry Review*, *Angles of Ascent: A Norton Anthology of Contemporary African American Poetry*, *At Length*, *The Believer*, *The Best American Poetry 2013*, *The Best American Poetry 2014*, *Boston Review*, *Connotation Press: An Online Artifact*, *Copper Nickel*, *Fence*, *Harvard Review*, *Indiana Review*, *The Iowa Review*, *jubilat*, *The Kenyon Review*, *Memorious*, *The Missouri Review*, *New Madrid*, *The New Republic*, *The New Yorker*, *Oxford American*, *Ploughshares*, *A Public Space*, *The Rumpus*, *Tin House*, *Transition*, *The Volta*, *Vinyl Poetry*, and *Weber—the Contemporary West*.

This book was written with the support of the Bread Loaf Writers' Conference, Cave Canem, Emory University, the Mrs. Giles Whiting Foundation, the National Endowment for the Arts, the Radcliffe Institute for Advanced Study at Harvard University, and the University of San Diego.

One's lover—or one's brother, or one's enemy—
sees the face you wear, and this face can elicit the
most extraordinary reactions.

JAMES BALDWIN

Contents

III

The New Testament

I

Colosseum

I don't remember how I hurt myself,
The pain mine
Long enough for me
To lose the wound that invented it
As none of us knows the beauty
Of our own eyes
Until a man tells us they are
Why God made brown. Then
That same man says he lives to touch
The smoothest parts, suggesting our
Surface area can be understood
By degrees of satin. Him I will
Follow until I am as rough outside
As I am within. I cannot locate the origin
Of slaughter, but I know
How my own feels, that I live with it
And sometimes use it
To get the living done,
Because I am what gladiators call
A man in love—love
Being any reminder we survived.

Romans 12:1

I will begin with the body,
In the year of our Lord,
Porous and wet, love-wracked
And willing: in my 23rd year,
A certain obsession overtook
My body, or I should say,
I let a man touch me until I bled,
Until my blood met his hunger
And so was changed, was given
A new name
As is the practice among my people
Who are several and whole, holy
And acceptable. On the whole
Hurt by me, they will not call me
Brother. Hear me coming,
And they cross their legs. As men
Are wont to hate women,
As women are taught to hate
Themselves, they hate a woman
They smell in me, every muscle
Of her body clenched
In fits beneath men
Heavy as heaven—my body,
Dear dying sacrifice, desirous
As I will be, black as I am.

Heartland

This is the book of three
Diseases. Close it, and you're caught
Running from my life, nearer its end now
That you've come so far for a man
Sick in his blood, left lung, and mind.
I think of him mornings
I wake panting like a runner after
His best time. He sweats. He stops
Facing what burned. The house
That graced this open lot was
A red brick. Children played there—
Two boys, their father actually
Came home. Mama cooked
As if she had a right to
The fire in her hands, to the bread I ate
Before I saw doctors who help me
Fool you into believing
I do anything other than the human thing.
We breathe until we don't.
Every last word is contagious.

Another Elegy

Expect death. In every line,
Death is a metaphor that stands
For nothing, represents itself,
No goods for sale. It enters
Whether or not your house
Is dirty. Whether or not
You are clean, you arrive late
Because you don't believe her
When, sobbing as usual, she
Calls to say if you don't stop
Your brother, she will kill him
This time. Why rush? By now,
You think she likes it, his hands
Slapping her seven shades of red.
Besides, your brother is much
Bigger than you—once you tried
Pulling him off the woman he loves
And lost a tooth. Expect to lose
Again as you stand for nothing
Over his body, witness
Or reporter, murderer or kin.

Cain

First, a conversation. Now,
A volcano. Call me quick-
Tempered vegan. Turnip
Lover. Fruit licker. Mound
Maker. Quiet. I can predict
An earthquake. I can cook
A rose. I'm first to kill
A weed. The collards
Should come quick this year.
The beans may be lean.
I plant seeds and wait
All winter to eat. Some
Slaughter sheep for dinner.
Some chew leaves. Firstborn
And patient, I give ground
Color. Pull pink from
Green. Azalea, vibrant
As a lamb's tongue. My kid
Brother killed one, but I
Dug the hole, soil still
Young, lava beneath it
Near each finger when little
Brothers tortured most
Of God's creatures, and small
Men watched them bleed.

Labor

I spent what light Saturday sent sweating
And learned to cuss cutting grass for women
Kind enough to say they couldn't tell the damned
Difference between their mowed lawns
And their vacuumed carpets just before
Handing over a five-dollar bill rolled tighter
Than a joint and asking me in to change
A few lightbulbs. I called those women old
Because they wouldn't move out of a chair
Without my help or walk without a hand
At the base of their backs. I called them
Old, and they must have been; they're all dead
Now, dead and in the earth I once tended.
The loneliest people have the earth to love
And not one friend their own age—only
Mothers to baby them and big sisters to boss
Them around, women they want to please
And pray for the chance to say please to.
I don't do that kind of work anymore. My job
Is to look at the childhood I hated and say
I once had something to do with my hands.

The Interrogation

I. WHERE

In that world, I was a black man.
Now, the bridge burns and I
Am as absent as what fire
Leaves behind. I thought we ran
To win the race. My children swear
We ran to end it. I'd show them
The starting point, but no sky here
Allows for rain. The water infects
Us, and every day, the air darkens...
The air, the only black thing
Of concern—
Who cares what color I was?

II. CROSS-EXAMINATION

Do you mean love?
Certainly a way of loving.

Did it hurt?
When doesn't it?

We'll ask the questions. Did it hurt?
When death enters a child's room,

The child feels a draft.
So you chose for it to hurt.

I chose my brother over my desire
To be invisible.

We thought your brother was dead...
He is.

And his death made you
Visible?

You only see me
When I carry a man on my back.

But you arrived alone.
That wasn't me.

That was the man who lost
My brother.

III. STREET DIRECTIONS

Will black men still love me
If white ones stop wanting me

Dead? Will white men stop
Wanting me dead? Will men

Like me stop killing men like
You? Which made us brothers—

That you shielded my body
With yours or that you found

Me here, dying on the pavement,
And held my empty hand?

IV. REDIRECT

Tell us, then, how did that man lose your brother?
I imagine

I lost him in the fire.
The record suggests

You lost him to a bullet.
The record was written

In my first language. The bullet is
How I lost myself.

And this preoccupation with color,
Was that before or after you lost yourself?

The women who raised me referred to Jesus
As "our elder brother."

And what about race?
What you call a color I call

A way.
Forgive us. We don't mean to laugh.

It's just that black is,
After all, the absence of color.

V. FAIRY TALE

Say the shame I see inching like steam
Along the streets will never seep
Beneath the doors of this bedroom,
And if it does, if we dare to breathe,
Tell me that though the world ends us,
Lover, it cannot end our love
Of narrative. Don't you have a story
For me?—like the one you tell
With fingers over my lips to keep me
From sighing when—before the queen
Is kidnapped—the prince bows
To the enemy, handing over the horn
Of his favorite unicorn like those men
Brought, bought, and whipped until
They accepted their masters' names.

Metal makes for a chemical reaction.
Now that my wrists are cuffed, I am
     Not like a citizen. What touches me
     Claims contamination. What
A shame. A sham. When the police come
They come in steel boots. Precious
     Metal. They want me kicked,
     So kick me they do. I cannot say
They love me. But don't they seek me out
As a lover would, each with both hands
     Bringing me to my knees, under God,
     Indivisible? I did not have to be born
Here. Men in every nation pray
And some standing and some flat
     On their backs. Pray luscious
     Silver. Pray Christmas. A chain
A chain. Even if it's pretty. Even around
The neck. I cannot say what they love
     Is me with a new bald fist in my mouth.
     Pray platinum teeth. Show me
A man who tells his children
The police will protect them
     And I'll show you the son of a man
     Who taught his children where
To dig. Not me. Couldn't be. Not
On my knees. No citizen begs
     To find anything other than forgiveness.

VII. LANDMARK

What Angel of Death flies by each house, waving

My brother's soul in front of windows like a toy—

A masked, muscle-bound action figure with fists

We wanted when we were children—some light

Item, a hero our family could never afford?

Paradise

That story I told about suffering
Was a lie. I never wandered
The woods with a box of matches.
Truth is I was born in the forest,
And there, I ran the weather.
Deer left apples in my hand, so
I didn't think to cook the deer.
The secret of my life was
My life, hair falling past my neck,
Beyond my back. I can't say
The nights grew cold, but Lord,
I was bored. What words I spoke
I yawned. And while I claimed
To have walked away hearing a voice
Or a fiddle, that too is untrue.
When a man leaves, he leaves looking
For more languages than there are
Tongues. When a boy leaves, we
Call him a man. You know that story
As well as you know my smile, how
It fit my face once I cut each tooth
In your well-wrought world, right
Along with this scar and this
One and this one and this...

To Be Seen

Forgive me for taking the tone of a preacher.
You understand, a dying man

Must have a point—not that I am
Dying exactly. My doctor tells me I'll live

Longer than most since I see him
More than most. Of course, he cannot be trusted

Nor can any man
Who promises you life for looking his way. Promises

Come from the chosen: a lunatic,
The whitest dove—those who hear

The voice of God and other old music. I'm not
Chosen. I only have a point like anyone

Paid to bring bad news: a preacher, a soldier,
The doctor. We talk about God

Because we want to speak
In metaphors. My doctor clings to the metaphor

Of war. It's always the virus
That attacks and the cells that fight or die

Fighting. Hell, I remember him saying the word
Siege when a rash returned. Here

I am dying while
He makes a battle of my body—anything to be seen

When all he really means is to grab me by the chin
And, like God the Father, say through clenched teeth,

Look at me when I'm talking to you.
Your healing is not in my hands, though

I touch as if to make you whole.

Langston's Blues

"O Blood of the River songs,
O songs of the River of Blood,"
      Let me lie down. Let my words

Lie sound in the mouths of men
Repeating invocations pure
      And perfect as a moan

That mounts in the mouth of Bessie Smith.
Blues for the angels kicked out
      Of heaven. Blues for the angels

Who miss them still. Blues
For my people and what water
      They know. O weary drinkers

Drinking from the bloody river,
Why go to heaven with Harlem
      So close? Why sing of rivers

With fathers of our own to miss?
I remember mine and taste a stain
      Like blood coursing the body

Of a man chased by a mob. I write
His running, his sweat: here,
      He climbs a poplar for the sky,

But it is only sky. The river?
Follow me. You'll see. We tried
      To fly and learned we couldn't

Swim. Dear singing river full
Of my blood, are we as loud under-
Water? Is it blood that binds

Brothers? Or is it the Mississippi
Running through the fattest vein
Of America? When I say home,

I mean I wanted to write some
Lines. I wanted to hear the blues,
But here I am swimming the river

Again. What runs through the fat
Veins of a drowned body? What
America can a body call

Home? When I say Congo, I mean
Blood. When I say Nile, I mean blood.
When I say Euphrates, I mean,

*If only you knew what blood
We have in common. So much,
In Louisiana, they call a man like me*

Red. And red was too dark
For my daddy. And my daddy was
Too dark for America. He ran

Like a man from my mother
And me. And my mother's sobs
Are the songs of Bessie Smith

Who wears more feathers than
Death. O the death my people refuse
      To die. When I was 18, I wrote down

The river though I couldn't win
A race, climbed a tree that winter, then
      Fell, flat on my wet, red face. Line

After line, I read all the time,
But "there was nothing I could do
      About Race."

'N'em

They said to say goodnight
And not goodbye, unplugged
The TV when it rained. They hid
Money in mattresses
So to sleep on decisions.
Some of their children
Were not their children. Some
Of their parents had no birthdates.
They could sweat a cold out
Of you. They'd wake without
An alarm telling them to.
Even the short ones reached
Certain shelves. Even the skinny
Cooked animals too quick
To catch. And I don't care
How ugly one of them arrived,
That one got married
To somebody fine. They fed
Families with change and wiped
Their kitchens clean.
Then another century came.
People like me forgot their names.

II

The Ten Commandments

But I could be covetous. I could be a thief.
Could want and work for. Could wire and
Deceive. I thought to fool the moon into
A doubt. I did some doubting. Lord,
Forgive me. In New Orleans that winter,
I waited for a woman to find me shirtless
On her back porch. Why? She meant it
Rhetorically and hit me with open hands.
How many times can a woman say why
With her hands in the moonlight? I counted
Ten like light breaking hard on my head,
Ten rhetorical whys and half a moon. Half-
Nude, I let her light into me. I could be last
On a list of lovers Joe Adams would see,
And first to find his wife slapping the spit
Out of me. I could be sick and sullen. I could
Sulk and sigh. I could be a novel character
By E. Lynn Harris, but even he'd allow me
Some dignity. He loved black people too
Much to write about a wife whipping her rival
On a night people in Louisiana call cold.
He'd have Joe Adams run out back and pull
Her off of me. He wouldn't think I deserved it.

Homeland

I knew I had jet lag because no one would make love to me.
All the men thought me a vampire. All the women were

Women. In America that year, black people kept dreaming
That the president got shot. Then the president got shot

Breaking into the White House. He claimed to have lost
His keys. What's the proper name for a man caught stealing

Into his own home? I asked a few passengers. They replied,
Jigger. After that, I took the red-eye. I took to a sigh deep

As the end of a day in the dark fields below us. Some slept,
But nobody named Security ever believes me. Confiscated—

My Atripla. My Celexa. My Cortisone. My Klonopin. My
Flexeril. My Zyrtec. My Nasarel. My Percocet. My Ambien.

Nobody in this nation feels safe, and I'm still a reason why.
Every day, something gets thrown away on account of long

History or hair or fingernails or, yes, of course, my fangs.

Host

We want pictures of everything
Below your waist, and we want
Pictures of your waist. We can't
Talk right now, but we will text you
Into coitus. All thumbs. All bi
Coastal and discreet and masculine
And muscular. No whites. Every
Body a top. We got a career
To think about. No face. We got
Kids to remember. No one over 29.
No one under 30. Our exes hurt us
Into hurting them. Disease free. No
Drugs. We like to get high with
The right person. You
Got a girl? Bring your boy.
We visiting. Room at the W.
Name's D. Name's J. We DeeJay.
We Trey. We Troy. We Q. We not
Sending a face. Where should we
Go tonight? You coming through? Please
Know what a gym looks like. Not much
Time. No strings. No place, no
Face. Be clean. We haven't met
Anyone here yet. Why is it so hard
To make friends? No games. You
Still coming through? Latinos only.
Blacks will do. We can take one right
Now. Text it to you. Be there next
Week. Be there in June. We not a phone
Person. We can host, but we won't meet
Without a recent pic and a real name
And the sound of your deepest voice.

Football Season

But the game includes killing
Boys in another country.
At the end of this beer,
I pay a tax, make sure
They're dead. A man asks to change
The channel, unaware of his own safety.
Barflies look at him as if he's spilled
The final pint of ale. Loneliness
Is a practice. Like medicine.
Like law, the law of the land
Live in twenty-four time zones.
The last man standing is
The first one alone. Which of us
Is too drunk to stagger
Home? Not me. I can drink
A few more, see the Patriots
Or the Cowboys or another
Very long war right
Here on this stool, watching
My money work for me, the heat
Up and me comfortable enough
To complain about it.

The Rest We Deserve

Our walls are thin, and the man who won't say hello
Back to me in the morning as we lock ourselves out
Of our homes—won't even nod my way as black men
Do when they see themselves in you—sings "Precious,
Precious," the only song he must know, to the newborn
Other neighbors tell me is all he has left of a woman
Who died, went to rehab, or left him for another,
Depending on the fool telling the story and the time
Of day it gets told. I don't know why it bothers me.
I don't need him to love me the way he loves that child,
Pacing an apartment I imagine looks just like mine
With a baby in his arms, none of us allowed the rest
We deserve, him awful and off-key, her—is it a she?—
Shrill as any abandoned animal should be. I want
To hurt him, and I want to help. I think of knocking
To say he doesn't have to be polite to me, but he should
Try stuffing the kid in a drawer and closing it; or
Knocking to show him the magic made when you sit
An infant in a car seat on top of a washer while you do
A little late-night laundry. Why do I think he owes me,
That all the words to Jackie Moore's one hit make him
Mine enough not to mind some man he sees me kiss good-
Bye while he rolls his eyes, a baby strapped to his chest,
A tie around his neck, and me yawning because somebody
Wouldn't let me sleep, everyone wishing any voice in this
Building could sing for the thing growing in the smallest
Of us when we open our mouths at odd hours to shriek?

What the Holy Do

for Previn Keith Butler (1978–2009)

Back when I was God, I had friends.
We wrote our own Bible
And got thrown out of church.
Then I saw one of us again—a man
Pushing into him
From behind. He turned

His final face to the camera
Like a teenager coming
Upon a pimple in the mirror.
The lonely worship alone.
I search out such filth in the cathedral
Of my home, but this time,

With a sheet, I covered the screen.
That's what the holy do to the body
After shutting its eyes,
And that's this scribe's last vision
Of another poorly recorded life
As I talk to myself in late July, dragging

A fan behind me like an oxygen tank.

Reality Show

An editor... wrote back that she liked the "Negro" poems
best... requested that Gwendolyn [Brooks] approach
Knopf again when she had more of these.

AMY SICKELS

NEWS

It is like a love for men, this
Love of language, and we are
Men at war, says the news.
No matter how long we speak
English, English means not
To count us or to count us
Darkly, but I know what
I want and so does channel 4.
They give it to me, one heap
After another: soldiers who,
Following another battle, shed,
Sweat, and spit like fountains.

THE HOUSEWIVES

All dese negroes calln us cute
But aint nobody tryna pay de light bill

Brothas on both coasts sayin Damn you
Sexy But not one payin dis light bill

And here our grinnin asses go after each
Compliment
              Lettin de fine ones cop a feel

TALK SHOW

We can talk love
If you want,
Though I need fuel,
Need bread, bed,
And sex. I go
To my pocket
For change. One nickel
Fails me, so I find
Another, dead man
At my finger, monument
Against my thumb. Take,
For instance, our love.
Take or give it away,
Or sell it for all
I care, for the next
Nickel I pinch, not much
Money to debate or make
You stay long
Enough to turn on
The TV where we see
The real world done
And watch a man
Grin then run
A finger through
His enemy's hair.

THE BACHELOR

All dese negroes swear Im cute
But none of em payin dis light bill

Liars in Lithonia and doctors in Detroit say
Damn you sexy But dey wont pay dis light bill

Still my ass go grinnin after each
Goldtoothed word

                    I can feel feel feel

Willing to Pay

It's your face I wanted. Spent
Days at the dentist hoping
He'd hammer the smile right.
Your face and that thing
You do with your eyes
When I get you livid. Don't be
Flattered. Don't be afraid.
It's 1979 or so. I'm known
To lie about my age. My parents
Are trying again. How's that
For language, the moans
They made making me. If only
One of them lasted longer,
If they preferred the dog to some
Other position, then maybe I'd be
The same on both sides or
A babyface the rest of my life.
This is the night of a thousand
Noses. You want entertainment,
But how can I watch TV knowing
A guy cuter than me is getting paid
To wink, and I'm the one
Willing to pay? I wonder awhile
At football. At least, I'd have had
A lovely set of calves. Everybody
Who eats loves an athlete
Naked and newly showered.
What's fair? You got the face
And the body and the cameras
Calling while I got you
Waiting for me to put the *w*

Behind the *o* in words like
Now. Now look, I bought you
Something else, something perfect
For hanging on that wall you wanted
Up. The painter did the damnedest
Job pulling your lips close to mine.

Dear Dr. Frankenstein

I, too, know the science of building men
Out of fragments in little light
Where I'll be damned if lightning don't

Strike as I forget one
May have a thief's thumb,

Another, a murderer's arm,
And watch the men I've made leave
Like an idea I meant to write down,

Like a vehicle stuck
In reverse, like the monster

God came to know the moment
Adam named animals and claimed
Eve, turning from heaven to her

As if she was his
To run. No word he said could be tamed.

No science. No design. Nothing taken
Gently into his hand or your hand or mine,
Nothing we erect is our own.

Another Elegy

I want to relax, but it's April.
My students cross and un-

Cross bare legs, one thigh,
In turn, holding the other

Down. Each limb,
Every stem on Earth

At battle, studded
With buds, all cocked

To win as the world
Splits into its stains. I live

With a disease instead
Of a lover. We take turns

Doing bad things
To my body, share a house

But do not speak. We eat
What I feed. Spring is a leg

And can't be covered. One day,
I was born. That was long ago.

Motherland

Our mother swears the woman's nose is wide enough
To dam the Red River.

Our mother says you could drain a swamp through
The gap in Angel's teeth.

She's too bottom-heavy for her clothes. Even in a housedress,
She looks like a whore fit for music videos.

Our mother keeps asking why so many music videos
Are filmed at pools and beaches.

Mama doesn't care that Angel has two kids
Or that she dropped out of school before
Meeting my brother—and while I want someone
To say what a shame it is that she outdrinks
Our dad at Thanksgiving—Angel's looks are all

Our mother will criticize, turning watery eyes
From my brother to me,

Pray my other boy won't bring anybody as ugly home.
And I never do.

He was a fool for a tall woman, and Angel stood taller than him in any pair of shoes. He saw her the way children see the trees they climb, their mothers cussing down below.

After his car quit, I'd pick him up for work. He'd light his morning cigarette and fidget with my stereo for something repetitive, explicit—the kind of music born when we were, the one sound we had in common.

I shouldn't, but I'm thinking
About the woman who got shot
Fighting over that sweat-soaked
Headscarf Teddy Pendergrass threw
Into the crowd at one of those
Shows he put on for "Ladies
Only" the year I was born. How
Many women reached
Before the tallest two forgot
Their new fingernails matched
Purses and shoes? I'm no good.
I thought I'd be bored with men
And music by now, voices tender
As the wound Pendergrass could feel
When he heard what caused gunfire
Was a trick he rehearsed. Love,
Quick and murderous, bleeding
Proof of talent. He wanted to be
What we pay to see— Of course,
That's not special. I imagine
Someone who desires any
Worn piece of man must be
Willing to shoot or be shot.

As we veered onto Line Avenue, he stopped the music, *Sometimes, I call Angel those names. She throws forks and plates when I do.*

He got out of my car laughing, but with his head in the window like it was his last chance at giving advice, *It feels good to have a woman fine as she is so mad at you.*

Before he saw Eve, the serpent walked upright
     And climbed and crawled like a man with limbs.
He tangled himself in reaches for green, prized
     The curves of his quick and endlessly slim

Body. Days were years then. The woman spent
     Most days in giggles or gorged on something
Significant placed in her palms. The serpent
     Admired her wandering, her ease at being

Described, entered. No one wanted, but even that garden
     Grew against the ground's will, and this,
Child, I tell you since soon you'll grow and harden—
     No matter how low she seemed squatting to piss,

The damned snake couldn't stop staring, and she couldn't
     Understand—though he inched close enough
To whisper something wet and true. He needed to confront
     Her with what he knew, needed her stuffed

On a sweet that made her see herself, see him
     And every beast in the young world watching.

That wasn't the day she killed him. They fought and called the police on each other for years. Nobody paid any mind.

But if I turn too quick on Line with the worst music, I can hear him again, explaining the satisfaction of hurting a woman who's still there the next morning. I think that's why he loved Angel, ugly or fine. What man wouldn't love a woman like that? And why can't I?

1 Corinthians 13:11

When I was a child, I spoke as a child.
I even had a child's disease. I ran
From the Doberman like all children
On my street, but old men called me
Special. The Doberman caught up,
Chewed my right knee. Limp now
In two places, I carried a child's Bible
Like a football under the arm that didn't
Ache. I was never alone. I owned
My brother's shame of me. I loved
The words *thou* and *thee*. Both meant
My tongue in front of my teeth.
Both meant a someone speaking to me.
So what if I itched. So what if I couldn't
Breathe. I climbed the cyclone fence
Like children on my street and went
First when old men asked for a boy
To pray or to read. Some had it worse—
Nobody whipped me with a water hose
Or a phone cord or a leash. Old men
Said I'd grow into my face, and I did.

Hustle

They lie like stones and dare not shift. Even asleep, everyone hears in prison.
Dwayne Betts deserves more than this dry ink for his teenage years in prison.

In the film we keep watching, Nina takes Darius to a steppers ball.
Lovers hustle, slide, and dip as if none of them has a brother in prison.

I eat with humans who think any book full of black characters is about race.
A book full of white characters examines insanity—but never in prison.

His whole family made a barricade of their bodies at the door to room 403.
He died without the man he wanted. What use is love at home or in prison?

We saw police pull sharks out of the water just to watch them not breathe.
A brother meets members of his family as he passes the mirrors in prison.

Sundays, I washed and dried her clothes after he threw them into the yard.
In the novel I love, Brownfield kills his wife, gets only seven years in prison.

I don't want to point my own sinful finger, so let's use your clean one instead.
Some bright citizen reading this never considered a son's short hair in prison.

In our house lived three men with one name, and all three fought or ran.
I left Nelson Demery III for Jericho Brown, a name I earned in prison.

III

Another Elegy

This is what our dying looks like.
You believe in the sun. I believe
I can't love you. Always be closing,
Said our favorite professor before
He let the gun go off in his mouth.
I turned 29 the way any man turns
In his sleep, unaware of the earth
Moving beneath him, its plates in
Their places, a dated disagreement.
Let's fight it out, baby. You have
Only so long left—a man turning
In his sleep—so I take a picture.
I won't look at it, of course. It's
His bad side, his Mr. Hyde, the hole
In a husband's head, the O
Of his wife's mouth. Every night,
I take a pill. Miss one, and I'm gone.
Miss two, and we're through. Hotels
Bore me, unless I get a mountain view,
A room in which my cell won't work,
And there's nothing to do but see
The sun go down into the ground
That cradles us as any coffin can.

Obituary

Say I never was a waiter. Say I never worked
Retail. Tell the papers and the police, I wrote

One color and wore a torn shirt. Nothing
Makes for longevity like a lie, so I had a few

Fakes and stains, but quote me, my hunger
Was sudden and wanting. I waited, marked

Time with what heart-
Beats I could hear, bumped my head nodding

At home. Some boys walked to my bedroom
In boots. Some of me woke wheezing the next

Morning wherever snow didn't fall by the foot
In a day. Beyond that, a name. For proof, a finger

Pointing forward. When you measure the distance
Between this grave and what I gave, you'll find me

Here, at the end of my body and in love
With Derrick Franklin, gift of carnelian,

Lashes thick as a thumb. Some men have a mind
For marriage. Some never

Leave home. If the body is a corporation,
I was the guy in charge of blood, my man

The CEO of bone. He kept a scandal
In my pocket. I sucked in my gut because I wanted

The lights on. Should a fool come looking
For money, say I was a bag boy and a nanny.

Beyond that, a nation looking backward. A smile
That would shine like the last line of cocaine.

Psalm 150

Some folks fool themselves into believing,
But I know what I know once, at the height
Of hopeless touching, my man and I hold
Our breaths, certain we can stop time or maybe

Eliminate it from our lives, which are shorter
Since we learned to make love for each other
Rather than doing it to each other. As for praise
And worship, I prefer the latter. Only memory

Makes us kneel, silent and still. Hear me?
Thunder scares. Lightning lets us see. Then,
Heads covered, we wait for rain. Dear Lord,
Let me watch for his arrival and hang my head

And shake it like a man who's lost and lived.
Something keeps trying, but I'm not killed yet.

A Living

A scribble, a pat on the back—and no more
Itches. I should have been a doctor. Better,

A preacher, a man who calls men to lift
Hands in surrender disguised as praise.

Everyone loves Jesus. He saves. He's
A healer. I lose when my man is right:

I cannot pay an electric bill, mine or his,
One of us sick, the other sicker, neither

Knowing how to sew or salve a wound, only
How precise the sound of him punctured.

After the Rapture

veritas sequitur esse

Nobody drowned in the flood.
In the beginning, the sky could not fail.
The first raindrops took men

By surprise. Everyone died
Of shock. But when man was born
Again, he liked words enough

To see if *wilted* might indeed modify
Trees, so he drove toward an edge,
Ran out of gas, turned back

To look at the desert, and like a nation
Testing its best weapons
In locations empty, unmarked,

Vast, he shredded himself
With glass, spilled into and over
Unnameable stretches of land,

Concrete, water, hands. Then,
The real killing began. The cacti
Leaked and lost their needles. A few

Men prayed. And we prayed to win.

Hebrews 13

Once, long ago, in a land I cannot name,
My lover and my brother both knocked
At my door like wind in an early winter.
I turned the heat high and poured coffee
Blacker than their hands which shivered
As we sat in silence so thin I had to hum.
They drank with a speed that must have
Burned their tongues one hot cup then
Another like two bitter friends who only
Wished to be warm again like two worn
Copies of a holy book bound by words to keep
Watch over my life in the cold and never ever sleep

Angel

I'm nine kinds of beautiful,
And all my hair is mine.
The finest girl in Cedar Grove,
All my hair mine.
My mama jumped in a river,
So I don't mind dying.

Yes, she read the Bible,
Read all about war in heaven.
Mama named me Angel
To spite that war in heaven.
Ask how many fights I won
Before I turned seven.

When you got hips like these,
Men want to take advantage.
He called my hips a pair of shelves.
The fool tried to take advantage.
Police don't ever show until
A bullet does some damage.

A few rules are schoolhouse.
Others you learn in church.
I got one rule for my babies
When a kid steals their lunch:
If anybody hits you, hit him
Back. Never wait to punch.

Mama drowned, but before that,
She taught me how to punch.
She lost a love then killed herself,

But she taught me to punch.
I hear my man laughing above.
I hit back hard, now he won't hush.

Receiving Line

California, November 4, 2008

Whenever a man wins, other men form lines
To wring his right hand like a towel wet
With what we want after washing. None

Of us clean, we leave soot older than color
Caked in his palm, so the winner we waited for
Can't see his own life line. This is mine,

Suited, on time: *My name is Jericho Brown.*
I like a little blues and a lot of whiskey. I read
When my children let me. I write what I can't

Resist. I'm as proud of you as a well-built chest, and
I am in unlegislated love with a man bound
To grab for me when he sleeps. Take my right hand,

The one that wakes him, the one I use to swear—

Make-Believe

Somewhere between here and Louisiana, I changed
Clothes, each quarter I counted and counted on gone.

Women carry cartons and kegs, bananas and eggs.

I only need sugar, some smokes, a can of Coke
To get through the margins where I write,

Metaphor = tenor + vehicle, for children who beg

To touch my hair and ask if I play basketball.
Tomorrow, I will explain the word *brother*

Is how we once knew black as someone

Frowns, raising his freckled hand: *So, you don't
Have a brother?* Milk warms behind me. Babies

Begin to cry. I dig again, this time coming back

With lint. *I am not a liar,* I tell the cashier. The next
Day to my students I'll say, *No, I don't have a brother*

In the world. Myth is not make-believe. My

Mother and father had only one son. This,
My brother, is a metaphor. I am the tenor.

Brother is how you get to me if you are black

And you leave Louisiana and you lose what little
Tender you thought you had to spend, broke

With a line to remember, people who need to eat.

Found: Messiah

blog entry at The Dumb, the Bad, and the Dead

A Shreveport man was killed
When he tried to rob two men.

Decided he could make money

Easier stealing it.
Police responding to

Gunshots found Messiah

Demery, 27, shot once in the chest
Trying to rob Rodrigus

And Shamicheal. Rodrigus got

A gun, but police found
Some marijuana, so he's going to jail

Too. This story would have been nicer

With some innocent people involved,
But one less goblin is one

Less goblin is one less.

Another Angel

I found myself bound to Him and bound to His
Bidding. He left water without color and land
With no motion to mention but kept me going

Like a toy wound tighter than His one odd eye
When I failed to deliver a message on time.
He built bugs and beasts; I understood my

Sexlessness. He invented men and women;
I knew I had no father. He never told me
What I was, what He could be. So what—

Two boys in Oil City, Louisiana, complain
About their bodies, featherless, modeled after
The reflection He passes in streams. They got

Sick playing barefoot in mud, and they hate
Their symptoms. I am that kind of pain
Put to purpose but unloved, bound to the Lord—

He looks at those brothers, never noticing his own—
Bound like their strange sister told to bathe them
Once, filthy and feverish, they finally come home.

Eden

One winter, we decided to plunge, to swim or drown,
Bare-dicked and beautiful. Then we slept as if the town
Were warm, though before either of us got born, heroes
Thought to end all threats by building one final weapon.
We said what any man should when waking cold, his lover
Pressed against him close—*Promise,* and, *I could die this way.*

Let's celebrate, O ye gentlemen of Thunder Bay.
Show me a brick. A bottle. Knuckles and feet.
Put on a pair of Nikes made for catching prey.
Don't just scare me. Find your keys and beat
The limp out my wrists. I worked all Friday,
And this is North America, for God's sake, treat
Me like it, like I looked at you that able way
You look at women to prove yourselves straight.

Another Elegy

To believe in God is to love
What none can see. Let a lover go,

Let him walk out with the good
Spoons or die

Without a signature, and so much
Remains for scrubbing, for a polish

Cleaner than devotion. Tonight,
God is one spot, and you,

You must be one blind nun. You
Wipe, you rub, but love won't move.

At the End of Hell

So what if I love him,
The one they call bad,
The one they call black,
The one with the gap
In his teeth only I get
To see. What if I risk
Taking the head of death
Here in the dark, far
And deep, where
Burrowing beasts build
House after filthy house,
And nobody witnesses
My underworld gangster
Play kidnap, play Mama's
Baby turned queen, and
If I scream, *Pastel*—he
Swears he's sorry, unties
My feet. What if that's
Worth a few bruises
Better than the light
Called spring, and I love
It, every drop of God
Weeping over me.

Heart Condition

I don't want to hurt a man, but I like to hear one beg.
Two people touch twice a month in ten hotels, and
We call it long distance. He holds down one coast.
I wander the other like any African American, Africa
With its condition and America with its condition
And black folk born in this nation content to carry
Half of each. I shoulder my share. My man flies
To touch me. Sky on our side. Sky above his world
I wish to write. Which is where I go wrong. Words
Are a sense of sound. I get smart. My mother shakes
Her head. My grandmother sighs: He ain't got no
Sense. My grandmother is dead. She lives with me.
I hear my mother shake her head over the phone.
Somebody cut the cord. We have a long-distance
Relationship. I lost half of her to a stroke. God gives
To each a body. God gives every body its pains.
When pain mounts in my body, I try thinking
Of my white forefathers who hurt their black bastards
Quite legally. I hate to say it, but one pain can ease
Another. Doctors rather I take pills. My man wants me
To see a doctor. What are you when you leave your man
Wanting? What am I now that I think so fondly
Of airplanes? What's my name, whose is it, while we
Make love. My lover leaves me with words I wish
To write. Flies from one side of a nation to the outside
Of our world. I don't want the world. I only want
African sense of American sound. Him. Touching.
This body. Aware of its pains. Greetings, Earthlings.
My name is Slow And Stumbling. I come from planet
Trouble. I am here to love you uncomfortable.

Nativity

I was Mary once.
Somebody big as a beginning
Gave me trouble
I was too young to carry, so I ran
Off with a man who claimed
Not to care. Each year,
Come trouble's birthday,
I think of every gift people get
They don't use. Oh, and I
Pray. Lord, let even me
And what the saints say is sin within
My blood, which certainly shall see
Death—see to it I mean—
Let that sting
Last and be transfigured.

Apocrypha

The beginning and ending of "Langston's Blues" are from the conclusion of Terrance Hayes's poem "A Small Novel."

"Always be closing"—in "Another Elegy" (This is what our dying...)—was a favorite piece of advice Liam Rector gave to his poetry students. The line was made popular by a monologue in the film version of David Mamet's *Glengarry Glenn Ross*.

Cedar Grove, in the poem titled "Angel," is a neighborhood in Shreveport, Louisiana, bordered by Hollywood Avenue, 85th Street, Line Avenue (mentioned in "Motherland"), and Mansfield Road.

"Receiving Line" is set in California, November 4, 2008, when citizens directed the state's 55 electoral votes to Barack Obama, who became the first African American U.S. President. They also voted that day to pass Proposition 8, which eliminated the right of same-sex couples to marry.

About the Author

Jericho Brown is the recipient of the Whiting Writers' Award and fellowships from the Radcliffe Institute for Advanced Study at Harvard University and the National Endowment for the Arts. His first book, *Please,* won the American Book Award. Brown is originally from Shreveport, Louisiana, and is currently an assistant professor at Emory University.

Lannan Literary Selections

For two decades Lannan Foundation has supported the publication and distribution of exceptional literary works. Copper Canyon Press gratefully acknowledges their support.

LANNAN LITERARY SELECTIONS 2014

Mark Bibbins, *They Don't Kill You Because They're Hungry, They Kill You Because They're Full*

Malachi Black, *Storm toward Morning*

Marianne Boruch, *Cadaver, Speak*

Jericho Brown, *The New Testament*

Olena Kalytiak Davis, *The Poem She Didn't Write and Other Poems*

RECENT LANNAN LITERARY SELECTIONS FROM COPPER CANYON PRESS

James Arthur, *Charms Against Lightning*

Natalie Diaz, *When My Brother Was an Aztec*

Matthew Dickman and Michael Dickman, *50 American Plays*

Michael Dickman, *Flies*

Kerry James Evans, *Bangalore*

Tung-Hui Hu, *Greenhouses, Lighthouses*

Laura Kasischke, *Space, in Chains*

Deborah Landau, *The Last Usable Hour*

Sarah Lindsay, *Debt to the Bone-Eating Snotflower*

Michael McGriff, *Home Burial*

Valzhyna Mort, *Collected Body*

Lisa Olstein, *Little Stranger*

Roger Reeves, *King Me*

Ed Skoog, *Rough Day*

John Taggart, *Is Music: Selected Poems*

Jean Valentine, *Break the Glass*

Dean Young, *Fall Higher*

For a complete list of Lannan Literary Selections from Copper Canyon Press, please visit Partners on our website: www.coppercanyonpress.org

Poetry is vital to language and living. Since 1972, Copper Canyon Press has published extraordinary poetry from around the world to engage the imaginations and intellects of readers, writers, booksellers, librarians, teachers, students, and donors.

WE ARE GRATEFUL FOR THE MAJOR SUPPORT PROVIDED BY:

THE PAUL G. ALLEN
FAMILY FOUNDATION

Lannan

THE MAURER FAMILY
FOUNDATION

Anonymous

John Branch

Diana and Jay Broze

Beroz Ferrell & The Point, LLC

Janet and Les Cox

Mimi Gardner Gates

Gull Industries, Inc.
on behalf of William and Ruth True

Linda Gerrard and Walter Parsons

Mark Hamilton and Suzie Rapp

Carolyn and Robert Hedin

Steven Myron Holl

Lakeside Industries, Inc.
on behalf of Jeanne Marie Lee

Maureen Lee and Mark Busto

Brice Marden

Ellie Mathews and Carl Youngmann as
The North Press

H. Stewart Parker

Penny and Jerry Peabody

John Phillips and Anne O'Donnell

Joseph C. Roberts

Cynthia Lovelace Sears and Frank Buxton

The Seattle Foundation

Dan Waggoner

Charles and Barbara Wright

The dedicated interns and faithful
volunteers of Copper Canyon Press

To learn more about underwriting Copper Canyon Press titles,
please call 360-385-4925 ext. 103

The Chinese character for poetry is made up of two parts: "word" and "temple." It also serves as press-mark for Copper Canyon Press.

This book is set in Parable, designed for digital composition by Christopher Burke in 2002. Display type is set in Classica, designed by Thierry Puyfoulhoux. Book design and composition by VJB/Scribe. Printed on archival-quality paper.

CPSIA information can be obtained
at www.ICGtesting.com
Printed in the USA
LVHW042149230719
625065LV00005B/8